*An important source of happiness
comes from a feeling of
belonging to this world.*

# Thrive!

## Catching the Spirit of Personal Economics

by
Emanuel A. Frenkel, Ph.D.

DELTA VISTA
DAVIS, CALIFORNIA

Copyright © 2004 Emanuel Frenkel
Published by Delta Vista Press
Davis, CA 95616
www.deltavistapress.com

Editor: Cathy Dean, Author's Helper, Davis, CA
Publication design, camera-ready production, and project
    coordination: Jeanne Pietrzak, Graphic Gold, Davis, CA
Cover: Victor Pietrzak, Graphic Gold


Publisher's Cataloging-in-Publication
*(prepared by Quality Books, Inc.)*

Frenkel, Emanuel.
    Thrive! : catching the spirit of personal economics /
by Emanuel A. Frenkel.
    p.  cm.
    Includes index.
    LCCN 2004094205
    ISBN 097556210-X

    1. Finance, Personal.  2. Success.  3. Self-culture.
4. Economics.  5. Self-presentation.  6. Marketing.
I. Title.

HG179.F74 2004                     332.024'01
                                   QBI33-2082


Manufactured in the United States of America
10  9  8  7  6  5  4  3  2  1

for Polly, Philip, and Lena

# TABLE OF CONTENTS

### Part One:
### Understanding the Spirit
### of Personal Economics

Making an Effort and Getting "Things"
Building Your Own Economy
Always Wanting More
Specialization Occurs
Barter Appears
Competition Drives Quality and Innovation
Barter Makes Way for Money
Institutions Allow for Prosperity
Money Drives Diversity
To Get More Money, You Must Be More Productive
Stored Wisdom and Learning

# PREFACE

**A**RE YOU SATISFIED with your economic status? Do you truly enjoy your work? Do you feel you have gained the economic well-being you had hoped for?

If you answered, "No," to any of these questions, don't worry. Once you have caught the Spirit of Personal Economics, you will be able to shout a mighty "YES!" to all of them.

This book is an action plan for your personal economic success, a plan that combines both the principles of economics and the key elements of self-improvement. It is a guide to the attitudes and actions that will put you on the road to personal economic well-being, a well-being *deeper and more satisfying* than you could have ever imagined. Use this book as a positive self-improvement road map for your navigation, a road map that will help you reap the benefits of the infinite opportunities awaiting you. But be prepared. Your beliefs about yourself as a player in the economy may change dramatically as you read on.

# INTRODUCTION

Hold on tight! You are about to catch the Spirit of Personal Economics!

What *is* the Spirit of Personal Economics? It is a *way of thinking,* a way *so empowering* that when you catch it, you will:

* Find greater satisfaction in who you are.

* Develop a positive mental attitude about your role in the economy.

* Strengthen your desire to improve your *economic well-being* – not only the growth of your

material wealth, but also your physical, spiritual, and emotional wealth.

❦ Sharpen the ability to sell your skills and creations to others so that you can acquire the material goods you want and need.

❦ Understand that the material goods you buy are from people who, like you, are selling *their* skills and creations.

❦ Acquire the goods and services you desire without feeling guilty about being too "materialistic."

❦ View the world of material creations as a reflection of our true, natural selves, a reflection of our deepest needs.

❦ Work synergistically, in cooperation, with your community.

❦ See your own personal economic advancement in a way that benefits both you and others.

❦ Treat everyone with courtesy and respect along the way.

In Part One, **Understanding the Spirit of Personal Economics**, you will learn how to increase your well-being based on the way you participate in your community.

In Part Two, **Enjoying the Spirit of Personal Economics**, you will learn how to look at your consumption and use of things in a new and positive way. You will see the power you gain by investing in yourself, and you will learn how to maximize the benefits of selling your skills and talents – the products of all your hard work. You will also learn how to develop a positive feeling toward your own economic potential and toward the larger community in which your potential plays out.

Throughout the book, short activities build your skills to increase your personal economic satisfaction. Action checklists remind you of the main ideas. As you read, you will see how to strengthen your economic progress in a way that also brings you a feeling of solidarity with your community.

Now, let's get on with the adventure. After a foray into ice cream tasting, we will explore your role in the economy with you in the driver's seat. Then, we'll turn to the attitudes and actions necessary to catch the Spirit.

# Part One

UNDERSTANDING
THE SPIRIT OF
PERSONAL ECONOMICS

# 1

## HÄAGEN-DAZS

IMAGINE YOURSELF IN PARIS. It is almost midnight. You are strolling down the broad and well-lit Avenue des Champs-Elysées in the city's center. Scores of cafés are filled with customers. The vitality of the people on this vast Parisian artery sharpens your senses to the sights, sounds, and smells of the French capital.

You face a glass-walled façade with the letters "Häagen-Dazs" emblazoned upon it. The façade rises several floors to an impressive height. Through its glass, you see crowds of people who seem to be enjoying themselves. You hesitate for a moment, then decide to enter Häagen-Dazs in the expectation that, once inside, you will experience a similar joy.

Inside, you look at the sea of people sitting at small tables. Indeed, there is no question: this is a place of pleasurable experiences. Some people seem to be in reverie. Most talk with their tablemates. All eat ice cream. Waiters, scurrying across a wide seating area, deliver ice cream in a medley of sizes, textures, flavors, and toppings. The available choices create combinations of ice cream dishes numbering in the hundreds.

Already familiar with life on the Champs-Elysées, you know that, on many nights, the available seating space inside Häagen-Dazs cannot accommodate the enormous number of people who desire to eat ice cream. Even when sufficient warmth allows for more than fifty tables to be added to the outside patio, people must still wait in long lines for service.

You notice the diversity of the customers and

how their tastes are just as diverse. Each person appears to arrive with an intensely personal notion of what kind of ice cream is best. A child enters dreaming of a single vanilla scoop. A woman in her thirties orders three scoops of different flavors in a glass dish, topped off with caramel sauce and nuts. A man of respectable years expresses a desire for low-fat frozen yogurt with two candy toppings sprinkled on top. The preferences go on and on.

If you pay close attention to the conversations at Häagen-Dazs, you will recognize that the diversity of the crowd extends beyond ice cream preferences. There is an array of attitudes as well. Side-by-side with would-be philosophers, musing on the meaning of life, stock market brokers scan the paper, intent on making millions. Social revolutionaries debate on how to change the world. Earnest students take notes, while the idle rich discuss their evening plans. Factory workers arrive, as do tourists, academics, and diplomats. The young and the old alike come to Häagen-Dazs: planning birthdays, discussing politics, arranging business affairs, making lists, watching, and thinking in a world of ice cream sweets. Even the most solitary of souls is calmed by being there. Eating ice cream personally selected from an abundance of flavors, fat contents, and serving sizes causes an extraordinary leveling effect where everyone, no matter their age, class, race, background, or interest can enjoy the experience of Häagen-Dazs.

In response to the demand for ice cream, enterprising people, like those who founded Häagen-Dazs, offer a valuable service: the production of ice cream and the construction of a pleasant atmosphere for eating it. The existence of Häagen-Dazs and our efforts to consume its ice cream come from our desire to create and consume material objects.

Häagen-Dazs exists because of:

* Our need to gain satisfaction by purchasing things with our own hard-earned money.

* Our relentless urge to know contentment in our personal economy – our own personal financial "world" in which we choose how to earn, spend,

and save our money.

❧ Our daily drive for both material survival and a feeling of well-being.

So why is Häagen-Dazs important?

❧ If you can remember that places like Häagen-Dazs exist to satisfy our needs and that those needs are why people create and sell products and services in the first place, you can be reassured, even excited, about your own desire to acquire material goods.

❧ If you can remember that others have similar desires to acquire new items and services, you can tap into them, just as the creators of Häagen-Dazs ice cream did, and *create a product, service, or skill* that will satisfy the desires of others.

❧ When you create a useful product or service, or act in ways that others appreciate, you contribute to their sense of well-being while improving your own.

Keep these points in mind as you continue along your quest to catch the Spirit.

## ACTIVITY

➡ GO TO A LOCAL ICE CREAM OR COFFEE SHOP. LOOK AT THE PRODUCTS THE SHOP OFFERS. WHAT DESIRES ARE SATISFIED BY THE SHOP? WHAT DESIRES COULD BE FULFILLED BY THE SHOP, BUT ARE NOT? THINK OF TWO DESIRES THAT HAVE BEEN FULFILLED AND TWO DESIRES THAT REMAIN UNFULFILLED.

When you start thinking of what others need, you can find ways to satisfy others and benefit yourself simultaneously. This is called synergy or a synergistic relationship.

## THE SPIRIT OF PERSONAL ECONOMICS CHECKLIST

✓ You have begun to view the world through "economic eyes." Everywhere, people are producing and consuming. *Everywhere, there is an economy at work.*

## WHAT'S NEXT?

Up ahead, you will learn the basics of any economy. These basics will help you take advantage of the economic opportunities awaiting you. With this knowledge, you'll be one step closer to acquiring deeper personal economic satisfaction and success.

# 2

## THE ECONOMY AT WORK

TO BETTER UNDERSTAND how the economy works, let's go out to an island. In this elementary description of an economy, you will see what essential desires and actions propel us to create a material world. Exploration of the simple life on this island will reveal basic truths about any economy, about ourselves. Although you may feel you have already learned the basics, a quick look at this economy will help you understand the central motivation behind very natural human interactions.

## MAKING AN EFFORT
## AND GETTING "THINGS"

Let's pretend you are stranded alone on the island. You might begin by waiting for a miraculous delivery of food and the magical appearance of shelter. Of course, this type of activity can only go on for so long. You will speedily discover that this method of acquiring necessities does not work. After waiting fails, you will determine that you must work to acquire what you want. You will have to use your imagination, time, skills, and effort to obtain what you desire. *Without your acceptance of the direct relationship between making an effort and acquiring necessities, you cannot be happy on the island. In fact, you might not survive without that acceptance.* The discomfort of cold and the threat of starvation are your motivations to work.

## BUILDING
## YOUR OWN ECONOMY

Off to work you go! First, you look for a shelter – a hole in the ground, a thicket of leaves, anything.

Since you cannot find what you are after, you must figure out a way to build a shelter yourself. During all of this thinking, you get hungry, so you take the time to search for food. You forage through shrubs, maybe even devise a spear and a slingshot for meat.

You successfully build your shelter and obtain food. You now attack the next wish: warmer clothing for the winter night. While hunting animals, you discover that some of them offer raw materials for clothing in the form of furs. You decide to specialize in catching animals with thick coats until you satisfy your immediate clothing needs. With food, shelter, and suitable attire taken care of, you find yourself experimenting with the construction of simple fishing boats, tree houses for rodent-free sleep, and a game or two to enhance the enjoyment of your free time.

What you are doing on this island, without thinking much about it, is building your own economy. You are the only person on the island. You and your island are the entire economy. You hold every role – inventor, producer, seller, and buyer. You control all the goods and services on the island. As you consume, you undoubtedly become bored with the basic, essential items you produce for yourself, so you begin to produce different things that satisfy new desires. You hunt for new fruits and build boats that are more sea-worthy. You celebrate your one-year anniversary on the island with a party, complete with a bonfire, seafood, and an intoxicating beverage made by combining water with the seeds of island plants.

## Always Wanting More

Naturally, you will try to improve your lot. Even without a social structure influencing you, you will still work toward the deep-seated goal of material well-being. Even if you reach the point where you believe you have all the food, shelter, clothing, boats, and toys you need, you will still discover some new want that can add to your feeling of well-being. This new want could be as simple as the discovery of a painkilling plant to relieve an ache or as complex as the construction of a small hang glider with which to soar over the treetops. How about a hammock on the top of a hill? *No matter how well-off you become, you will always want something else to improve your well-being.*

## SPECIALIZATION OCCURS

What will happen if, instead, you find yourself on the island with other people? You will learn to share tasks. You and the islanders will follow your own inclinations as you begin to work for a better life. In time, some of you will make shelters, some will produce food, and others will fashion garments. You and the islanders will develop skills and become proficient in your own specific occupations. This is called *specialization of work*.

## BARTER APPEARS

A form of trade called barter will then arise on the island. Barter works as follows:

You determine that you have perfected a method of fashioning shelters from native leaves, grasses, and mud. You decide to specialize in the production of shelters while your compatriots engage in other occupations, such as hunting or making clothes.

In this situation, let's say you feel the need for warm blankets. Now you must find a blanket-maker who makes blankets to your liking. Then you must offer to trade a shelter for an agreed-upon number of blankets. You find a blanket-maker who wants one of your shelters. You strike an exchange deal. The agreement might be one blanket in exchange for one shelter. This deal is called barter trade, and the exchange establishes the price of a shelter on the island at one blanket.

For the moment, you are the only shelter-producer on the island. If many people want your structures, you may find another blanket-maker willing to offer you two blankets for your shelter. The more people willing to offer a higher quantity of blankets in exchange for one of your shelters, the more valuable your brand of shelters becomes.

# COMPETITION DRIVES QUALITY AND INNOVATION

If the value of your shelters continues to rise, inevitably, someone else will attempt to enter the shelter business to take advantage of the growing desire for new island dwellings. The desire to gain wealth and profit drives the new entrant into your line of business. The price of a single shelter may be four blankets by this time.

Now you face competition. In this case, you must make some production decisions in order to see your business prosper. Quite likely, new shelter-producers will establish a lower shelter price to steal away your existing customers and ensure a steady flow of clients for themselves.

In order for you to keep your price steady at four blankets – and to keep your customers – you may consider offering new, improved shelter features, such as multiple entrances or thicker walls. With these changes to your product, you increase the usefulness of your shelters without asking for more blankets in exchange.

You also try alternative strategies. You consider lowering your shelter prices to attract buyers for your existing shelter styles. But as soon as you encourage sales by lowering prices, you must follow up on this decision by determining ways to construct shelters with less time and effort to keep your profits high. Justifying the lower prices will motivate you to become more efficient at shelter production.

## BARTER MAKES WAY FOR MONEY

Up until now, the island economy has depended on barter exchange; however, it will not last for long. After your first sale of a shelter for the price of one blanket, you may feel that you have enough blankets. But what if the only people interested in acquiring shelters are blanket-makers? What if the food-gatherers prefer to sleep under the stars or, during bad weather, the shelter of a cave? How will you obtain the things you want?

*Exchange by barter breaks down because it*

*becomes impossible to match the personal needs of each islander with what each produces.* At the present time, you may want one blanket, one spear, one hammer, and a three-day supply of intoxicating plant-based beverage. In addition, you crave that hill hammock. For shelter, the hammock-maker uses a bag made of animal skin tied between two trees and, for the moment, is content with this structure.

You determine that, for the cold nights on the island, the hammock-maker wants the latest portable heater – beeswax in a conch shell. You decide to build such a heater, which you intend to trade for a hammock. But you quickly discover that you don't know the first thing about obtaining beeswax nor can you find the right type of shell. Also, you cannot compete with the regular makers of portable heaters whose work quality and cost efficiency far surpass your own.

Furthermore, as the essential needs for food, shelter, and clothing are met on the island, you and the islanders demand both improvements to existing products and the creation of new products. In response to the demand, you and the islanders will want to produce more interesting products. *The islanders' demand for improvements and new products will drive efforts to supply such products.*

Now the islanders want to consume shelter, food, and clothing in styles that none could have dreamed of before. Barter trade can no longer support the diverse desires of the islanders. To help the expansion of this economy, a uniquely human invention appears: money.

Over thousands of years, money has been described in many ways, some positive, some negative. *But one thing about money is certain: it is an absolute necessity for economic prosperity.* With money measuring the value of traded commodities, the islanders will be able to invent, make, buy, sell, and use products in varieties and styles that would be impossible with barter exchange.

# Institutions Allow for Prosperity

On the island, money appears as special leaves with numeric notations scratched upon them. As the island becomes more sophisticated, and you and the islanders accept the usefulness of money, the community establishes an authority, or government, vested with the power to control the number of special leaves on the island and to ensure the difficulty of counterfeiting them.

The authority will eventually learn how to control the number of leaves in circulation on the island so that the amount of leaves on the island expands with the increasing number of commodities (material goods and services). When this happens, a remarkable thing occurs. You and the islanders will respect money and the goods and services that money buys. Goods and services will be bought and sold in accordance with the rules of money, following the numeric values placed on each leaf. Islanders will also respect money payments they receive in exchange for their ability to produce valuable work or products. Money will become the accepted measure of value for all the goods and services sold on the island.

Money has become the standard measurement of wealth and a symbol of value. These qualities of money will push the islanders to desire enough money so they feel that they have a specific, if not growing, amount of wealth. You will also feel this desire.

## MONEY DRIVES DIVERSITY

What is your wealth on the island? Your wealth is your money and all your material possessions, self-made or purchased. Since all things on the island exchange for a current value of money, the items you possess have a value equal to the current prices for them. If people covet new shelters more than the older versions, the new shelters will be worth more than older models. If people think the older shelters are of a higher quality, then older shelters may command a greater money value than many of the more recent arrivals.

You and the islanders have invented money to help the island economy expand, an expansion caused by a kaleidoscope of desires for more diverse products and services. *Seen in this light, money is a basic expression of improvement for the individual and the community.* With money in the economy, you can sell shelters to your customers without needing their goods. You can take money from your shelter sale and buy the new hammock you want from the hammock-maker who sleeps between the trees. *Money furthers a more diverse, efficient, and growth-oriented economy; it drives innovation.*

## To Get More Money, You Must Be More Productive

The more money you have in your hand, the greater command you'll have over goods and services, should you want to acquire them. What becomes increasingly important is your realization that *money will buy the work and services of your fellow islanders.* With money, you can either buy the work of other people indirectly, by buying their products, or you can hire them directly to do things for you. People will give you a full-body massage, the chance to fly in a hang glider, or serve you a prepared meal for money. People will help you build your shelters for money. They will even serve you intoxicating plant-based beverages.

In addition, there will be some people who will like you, be attracted to you, appeal to you for advice, and grant you favors simply because you have money. When the full realization of this essential fact hits most of us, the reaction is very normal: we want more money. So how can we get it?

If you look at human history, you will see that *the only way to consistently get more money is to be useful to others in your community.*

You have no choice in this matter. The island economy will grow. This will occur because there are always people who will use their minds creatively to be of service to others. For example, it will not be long before one of the shelter-makers adds novel features to new shelters, commanding higher prices. Or this shelter-maker may determine that it is possible to sell more shelters with newer features at the existing price. Either way, the shelter-maker tries to be more useful to the buyers of shelters. More shelters sold at the existing prices or better models sold at higher prices means more money for the shelter-maker.

Thus, no matter in what occupation you find yourself, you will meet people in your profession who strive to improve their wealth by making themselves more useful. *If you want to increase your own wealth and thus protect your own ability to consume on the island – and in the "real world" – you must do the same.*

## Stored Wisdom and Learning

Throughout this story, an important process has occurred: the accumulation, or gathering, of wisdom and experience. As the island economy grows, this vast store of knowledge occupies the collective mind and passes with increasing efficiency from person to person. In fact, whole industries develop in order to pass on this information. Schools, occupational organizations, and teachers become the storehouses of knowledge on this island. This knowledge will never be lost. From it springs new ideas, concepts, and inventions. This knowledge manifests itself in the medicine, methods of education, and learned cooperation on the island.

At any stage of this island story, energetic people seize this stored knowledge daily to create new and improved products and services. These people utilize knowledge to gain a profitable advantage. They continually transform know-how into useful technology. In this way, knowledge shapes the products the islanders create.

With time, new products become old products, and you and the islanders become restless. *Very basic to your makeup, you and the islanders desire novelty. To invent the new, you and the others draw on the "storehouse" of knowledge to produce new goods and services for the island community.* A variety of new products appears: cups and saucers to handle beverages, spring-loaded crossbows, games combining cards and dice, long boards fashioned from fallen trees for something called surfing.

In the context of our own "real world," the yearning for knowledge and our ability to use that knowledge to our advantage has paid off over centuries, and it will continue to pay off in the future. We see the use of knowledge in how we have increased our physical comfort and in our ceaseless attempts to overcome challenges as they arise. Our knowledge has led to advances as simple as cooking a meal and as complex as isolating vaccines against disease.

Today, our island has become a huge global economy. In the global economy, challenges abound. These range from increasing food output in barren soil to the need for non-polluting transportation. Later, we will see the implications of our drive to overcome such problems as well as your own role in solving them.

From this island economy, you have learned the basic motivations of our quest for material well-being and personal economic satisfaction:

※ On the island, you accept that there is a direct relationship between making an effort and acquiring necessities. The discomfort of cold and the threat of starvation motivate you to work.

※ You build your own economy when you are alone on the island. You hold every role – inventor, producer, seller, and buyer.

※ Even without a social structure to influence you, you will still work toward the deep-seated goal of material well-being, and, no matter how well-off you are, you will always want something else.

※ With others on the island, specialization of work occurs.

※ Then, barter appears.

※ With competition, you improve your product or service to stay profitable.

※ Exchange by barter breaks down because it becomes impossible to match the personal needs of the individual islanders with what is produced.

❦ Money is invented.

❦ Money facilitates a more growth-oriented economy; money drives innovation.

❦ To accumulate more money, you must become more useful to other people in your community.

❦ Wisdom accumulates, allowing for a growing economy.

For clarity, refer to the diagram on the next page:

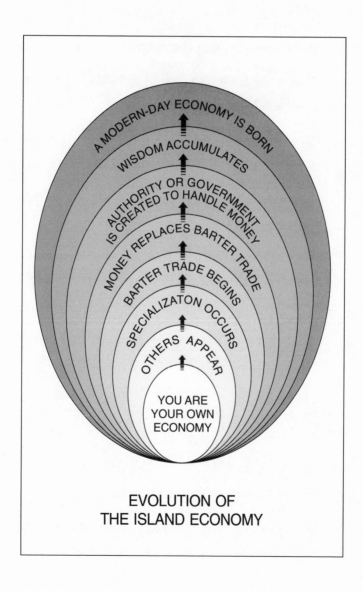

EVOLUTION OF
THE ISLAND ECONOMY

## ACTIVITIES

→ HOW IS YOUR COMMUNITY SIMILAR TO THE IS-
LAND SCENARIO?

→ LOOK AT YOUR DAILY ROUTINE. WHEN AND HOW
DO YOU ACT AS A PRODUCER? AS A CONSUMER?

→ IN WHAT WAYS ARE YOUR SKILLS AND WORK EFFORTS
USEFUL TO OTHERS?

→ CAN YOU THINK OF WAYS TO INCREASE YOUR USE-
FULNESS TO OTHERS?

→ CAN YOU THINK OF WAYS THAT THE ACCUMULATED
KNOWLEDGE AND WISDOM IN YOUR COMMUNITY HELP
YOU IN YOUR WORK?

## THE SPIRIT OF PERSONAL ECONOMICS CHECKLIST

✓ You have learned a practical example of how
you and others fit into an economy.

✓ You have learned the basic motivations that
create an economy. You see the reasons for the

existence of money, for the constant drive of people to improve their products and services with new technologies, and for the desire to accumulate wealth.

✓ You have seen how everyone interconnects with everyone else to create an economy.

Remember, our unyielding urge to improve our well-being and diversify our lives is a positive force that has created the material world and our economy.

## WHAT'S NEXT?

Now, we can take a closer look at your own personal economy. In the chapters to come, you will learn how to hone your attitude and skills in order to earn purchasing power over the goods and services you desire. You will learn how to catch the Spirit of Personal Economics to both benefit from and contribute to your community.

# 3

## CATCHING THE
## SPIRIT OF
## PERSONAL ECONOMICS

A S SOON AS THE ISLANDERS SOUGHT to improve their economic well-being, the opportunities for economic advancement appeared. Seizing these opportunities, the islanders found ingenious ways of being useful to others. But behind all their hard work, a constant reality remained: the passage of time.

## THE INDISPENSABLE RESOURCE

In any economy, time is the one indispensable resource available to each person. But, for each person, time has a limit: only so many hours in a day, only so many days in a year, only so many years in a lifetime. Learning to use this limited resource constructively will help you catch the Spirit – you'll be on your way to personal economic growth and contentment.

You have no choice in the matter of time. Your actions must occur in the passage of time as time marches on relentlessly. Each of us, faced with this immutable fact, must answer the same questions: What am I going to do with the time that I have? And how am I going to act as the time that I do possess moves onward? As far as your personal economics go, you want to make the best of your circumstances and feel as if you spent your time well. How do you do this?

An examination of your options in the economy will help you. When you have options, you have the opportunity to make decisions. In your personal economy, many of your decisions will revolve around how to move forward in time from your present situation. Once having decided on a plan of action, you will then make many decisions on how you will carry out this plan.

In a quest to catch the Spirit and make good use of your resource of time, you must:

* Understand the power of goal-setting and adhere to your goals regardless of any challenges you may face.

* Develop a positive attitude to meet each challenge with a steady mind.

* Harness your constructive impulses to advance, serve, and exchange.

* See work as your link to the community and a potential source of happiness.

* Discover a way to work that makes you and others happy.

## GOALS AND OBJECTIVES

Unfortunately, we must confront the constraint of time in our drive to reach our goals. Time moves forward without beginning or ending. And for a limited period, we are here. By assigning importance to moments during that period in which we live, we give meaning to our lives.

We all associate ourselves with significant points of time. For you, these moments might be birthdays, religious observances, the initial moments of a dream job, the first day fully recovered from surgery, or a first kiss. *We give meaning to our position in time by formulating plans to create significant moments. Thus, the fixing of goals takes center stage.*

Before we continue, put yourself into a goal-setting mindset and place yourself on a positive personal economic pathway. Follow the activities below.

## ACTIVITIES

➡ WHAT ARE YOUR CURRENT ECONOMIC AND LIFE GOALS? ARE YOUR GOALS SHORT TERM OR LONG

TERM? YOUR GOALS COULD INCLUDE THE ACQUI-
SITION OF SOMETHING MATERIAL, SUCH AS A LARGER
HOME OR A SMALLER CAR. YOUR GOALS COULD BE
PHYSICAL ATTRIBUTES, SUCH AS POWERFUL LEGS OR A
SLOW HEARTBEAT. YOUR GOALS COULD BE FINAN-
CIAL, EDUCATIONAL, OR RELATED TO SPIRITUAL
ENHANCEMENT, SUCH AS MASTERING THE ART OF
MEDITATION. YOUR GOALS COULD BE AS LONG TERM
AS TRAINING FOR THE ASCENT OF MT. EVEREST
OR AS SHORT TERM AS WAKING UP EARLY TO GO
RUNNING. WRITE YOUR TOP FIVE GOALS.

➡ ARE YOUR GOALS GOING TO CHALLENGE YOU? HAVE
YOU SET GOALS YOU TRULY WANT TO ACHIEVE? WILL
YOU REALLY FEEL GOOD ABOUT ACHIEVING THESE
GOALS? IF NOT, CHANGE YOUR GOALS. MAKE THEM
MOTIVATING.

➡ HOW COULD YOU FURTHER YOUR GOALS TODAY?
WOULD YOU MAKE A LIST? WRITE THAT LETTER?
BUY A BOOK? BOOK A FLIGHT? ACT UPON ONE OR
SEVERAL OF YOUR GOALS TODAY.

# A Simple Example
## of Goal-Setting

Once you have sighted your objective, you have declared to yourself, "In the future, I shall reach that destination." You will arrive at your destination by progressing in steps, using resources you find, taking opportunities that arise, finding people who can be of assistance, and harnessing your own thinking power. If you meet with pitfalls along the way, you will change your tactics instead of giving up. Let's look at an example of this process:

You decide you need to go out to buy a box of cereal for your morning breakfast. You choose to drive your car to the supermarket, where you will buy your cereal. Your goal is to bring the cereal home and eat some. Your mouth waters. You've set your goal. You need to use several resources at hand to achieve your goal, including the time it will take to employ those resources. In this simple case, your resources may be the money in your wallet, a car, paved streets, shopkeepers, and the supermarket itself. In your mind, you have fixed the goal and have a fairly good idea about what the most probable circumstances will be during the next twenty minutes as you try to achieve it. You get in your car, start the engine, and head off.

But wait. There's a house fire in your neighborhood. Firemen have blocked a key road. You have to take an alternative route. When you arrive at the supermarket, the electricity has been disconnected and the shopkeeper has temporarily closed it. On the way to another supermarket, your tire goes flat.

You had not envisioned these events in your initial picture of how to reach your goal. You may feel frustrated. At this point, adopting a positive attitude and feeling confident that you will get your cereal will help you achieve your goal quicker and with fewer internal struggles.

You decide to take thirty minutes at a gas station to fix the tire. Finally, at the second supermarket, you obtain just the cereal you set out to get. You return home and enjoy your bowl of cereal. You have met your objective, and you have just spent an hour of time on a quest that gives direction to this point of your existence. You responded to your desire to eat cereal. On your mission, you interacted with the community and creatively dealt with challenges as they arose. You reacted to each turn of events with ingenuity. You took an alternative route. You decided to try another store. Such persistence will win in the end with any goal.

The same principles apply any time you are trying to achieve something. This something could be earning a college degree, building a model airplane, washing clothes, mastering a piano concerto, or accumulating a million dollars. The routes are the same:

* You pick a goal or achievement.

* You imagine its outcome.

* You develop a plan of attack.

* You change your plans as you face challenges and take alternative routes when unexpected events bar your way.

* You do not give up.

All human achievements, from the baking of bread to landing on the moon, have followed this sequence. Taking these steps gives meaning to our lives as time passes.

Imagine if you did not fix goals. Without objectives on which to pin dreams, you would float randomly through time. Without goals, you would have no direction.

As you deploy what resources you have and what assets you are able to gain on your quest, take advantage of the many circumstances the world has to offer. In pursuing your goal, you will get the opportunity to cooperate with the world outside yourself.

In the economy, the importance of goals cannot be underestimated. On a personal level, you measure your achievement, an important yardstick of success, based on the accomplishment of your goals. In the community, the invention of ice cream, medical advancements, and the creation of the luxury car are examples of goals achieved. None of these achievements happened purely by accident. These accomplishments came from people just like you, reacting to wants and needs of the community, and their accomplishments have given shape to rising standards of living.

Goals are important. As we go through life, the goals we set for ourselves provide meaning to the passage of our lives. Through our goals, we can envision what the future may hold, and, in that future, we can see the realization of our hopes for improvement.

To adhere to your goals, remember:

〰 Time is the one indispensable resource available to everyone.

〰 By assigning importance to moments in which you live, you give meaning to your life.

〰 You will arrive at your destination by progressing in steps, using all available resources. If you meet with pitfalls along the way, you will change your tactics instead of giving up.

❧ Pursuing a goal places you in a situation in which you cooperate with your community.

## THE POSITIVE MENTAL ATTITUDE

Along with understanding the power of goals, you must also understand the importance of a positive mentality. If you don't already have this mentality, you want to get into the habit of adopting an optimistic perspective. *When you have a positive mental attitude, you have an outlook that everything will progress toward a beneficial result.* This outlook also holds that the kindness of other people will support you in times of need, and that, ultimately, you will prevail on your quest. *This outlook will be the deciding factor between accomplishing your goals and quitting.*

Perhaps you still don't believe that there's anything worth viewing optimistically. You may be a pessimist at heart. The transition to optimism will require a little work, but the results are astounding.

Think of it this way. The world can be viewed as a bad place or a good place. *The key is to view it in a way that will benefit you.* When you meet challenges that stand in the way of your goal, you need to be optimistic. If you don't believe that you can accomplish your goal, what will keep you from giving up? Nothing. That's why it's so important for you to look at the world and your role in it with positive expectations. With optimism, you have a better chance of persevering.

Most of us are good, reasonable human beings. Of course, the exceptions hit the front page, and in this respect, the news does a very good job of informing us. Even if we accept that much of human history involves tyranny, shouldn't we decide here and now, despite (or because of) our ugly history, to create a better life for ourselves? Shouldn't we focus on those people who try to make the best possible circumstances for themselves and others? Shouldn't we strive to be one of those people, too?

For example, an airplane crash occurs in which hundreds lose their lives. Immediately, an outpouring of sympathy follows. An army of volunteers combs the wreckage for clues to the cause of the crash. Airlines ground planes with a similar design, churches hold memorial services in honor of the victims, and many work long hours for weeks on end to determine the cause in an effort to forestall the next crash. The help and care coming from thousands express our essentially positive nature. The typical reaction to a disaster that involves human suffering is the cooperation of good-hearted people trying to make the best of a bad situation. We accept as a matter of fact that people will respond to others in need. What's more, most of us get a rush of positive feelings when we help others.

In order to plan and set goals, in order to see the passage of time as more than an endless road to nothingness, you *must* be optimistic. You must believe that your goals can be reached and that your goals make sense. You must expect that other people will be able to teach you the skills you need to reach your goals.

## THE MATERIAL WORLD
## POSITIVELY AFFECTS
## WORLD ISSUES

To ask that you maintain a positive mental attitude as you improve your own economic well-being *should not and will not* diminish your concern with the important issues we face. Your drive for economic well-being is a fact of life, but it is a trait that, once aligned with the Spirit of Personal Economics, will put you in a *stronger position* to address world issues and concerns.

Take the example of a photographic exposé project on the working conditions of Brazilian gold miners. Even when confronted with the harsh poverty of the miners, we can be thankful for the goods, services, and personal economic successes that brought this to our attention. Without cameras, lenses, film, air travel, inoculations against tropical disease, rugged denim jeans, and the tools of publishing, getting this important information to the wider public, with an intent to bring reform, would be hard indeed. To bring important issues to light, everyone relies on the material world. In fact, new technology and products make worldwide political awareness possible. Today, men and women with a positive outlook strategize to eradicate poverty and human discomfort with a host of ideas and goals, aided by a vast array of products and services.

How can you learn to be more optimistic? How can you develop this positive perspective? Think about ways you can:

🌣 Contribute to the community in a way that benefits others *and* improves your own self-esteem.

🌣 Strengthen your own personal economic well-being and, in turn, strengthen your impact in helping to alleviate some of the most vexing world issues.

🌣 Develop the outlook that everything will progress toward a beneficial result.

🌣 See optimism and achievement as an essential part of our human spirit.

# ACTIVITIES

➡ BE AWARE OF YOUR THOUGHT PROCESS FOR THE DAY. DO YOU HAVE ANY PREVAILING NEGATIVE PHRASES IN YOUR SPEECH, SUCH AS, "I CAN'T," "YEAH, BUT," OR "IT'S NOT GOING TO WORK"? ASK A FRIEND OR FAMILY MEMBER TO HELP YOU RECOGNIZE IF YOU USE ANY NEGATIVE PHRASES. THINK OF ALTERNATIVE POSITIVE PHRASES TO REPLACE THE NEGATIVE ONES AND WRITE THEM DOWN. EXCHANGE YOUR NEGATIVE PHRASES WITH YOUR NEW POSITIVE ONES.

➡ WHEN SOMETHING BAD HAPPENS TO YOU, NOTICE YOUR THOUGHT PROCESS. ARE YOU THINKING ABOUT HOW THE SITUATION CAN HELP YOU? THINK OF HOW YOU CAN VIEW THE SITUATION IN A MORE POSITIVE LIGHT. WHAT CAN YOU LEARN FROM THE BAD EVENT? IF YOU ARE HAVING TROUBLE THINKING OF A POSITIVE BENEFIT, ASK AN OPTIMISTIC FRIEND TO TELL YOU HOW THEY VIEW YOUR SITUATION.

➡ THINK ABOUT A WORLD ISSUE THAT AFFECTS YOU.

IS IT HUNGER, POVERTY, WAR, ENVIRONMENTAL POL-
LUTION? THINK ABOUT THE IMPACT YOU HAVE
ON THAT ISSUE RIGHT NOW AND WHAT OTHERS ARE
DOING TO ADDRESS THIS ISSUE USING THE MATERIAL
WORLD, TECHNOLOGIES, AND STORED-UP WISDOM AS
THEIR RESOURCES. CONSIDER YOUR OWN RESOURCES
AT HAND. WHAT KIND OF POSITIVE IMPACT COULD
YOU HAVE IF YOUR ECONOMIC WELL-BEING ALLOWED
YOU TO LOBBY IMPORTANT LAWS THROUGH CON-
GRESS? OR IF YOU HAD ENOUGH MONEY TO DONATE
A LARGE SUM IN ORDER TO START A NEW SCHOOL IN
AN IMPOVERISHED AREA? OR ENOUGH TO BRING
CHRISTMAS PRESENTS TO THE POOR? WRITE DOWN
WHAT YOU WOULD DO FOR THE WORLD IF YOUR
ECONOMIC WELL-BEING ALLOWED YOU TO MAKE
A HUGE IMPACT ON PEOPLE'S LIVES. THEN WRITE
FIVE WAYS IN WHICH, USING YOUR CURRENT RE-
SOURCES, YOU CAN IMPACT YOUR COMMUNITY.
FOLLOW THROUGH ON ONE IDEA TODAY.

## KNOW THE THREE DRIVES
## THAT EMPOWER YOU

Goals and optimism, though integral to the Spirit of Personal Economics, must also work in tandem with the active use of vital human impulses. To make full use of your options in the economy, three of these impulses must be accepted as integral to human progress. They are:

ꙮ The drive to advance.

ꙮ The drive to serve.

ꙮ The drive to exchange.

These three drives motivate us. When working together, they become building blocks for personal economic success and contentment.

At birth, you are blessed with the seeds of these impulses. At any time, they have the potential to develop for your benefit. As you journey through life, it becomes your choice whether or not you will use them together effectively to attain a sense of well-being. Of equal importance, you must accept that virtually everyone in your community has the potential to act upon these three impulses in ways that will be helpful to you.

## THE DRIVE TO ADVANCE

We begin with the drive to advance. When you have the drive to advance, you have the motivation to improve, to gain knowledge, and to be successful. This drive is a positive attribute of human behavior basic to our survival. In fact, the improvements in our world and much of our daily behavior come from our drive to advance. To survive in any environment, the impulse to improve forces us into action. Everyone wants to eat, have shelter, be clothed, and have the best medical care when needed. For as long as we have tracked human history, people have made consistent efforts to satisfy these wants in new and improved ways.

Games are an example of our drive to advance put to action. Virtually everyone around the globe loves to watch and participate in games. Games can be as simple as tossing a ball between two people to see who drops the ball first. Games can be complicated, like chess or baseball. But all games claim advance as their objective. All are based on survival and achievement. A baseball team strives to win a World Series, a chess player to checkmate an opponent. All games are rooted in the drive to advance.

Also, consider the following:

Few young adults today would consider spending four or more years in college unless inwardly they felt that there was something to be gained from the experience. This expectation could be a sense of greater flexibility in the job market. It could be the feeling of empowerment that comes from excelling in a specific subject. It could be a straightforward desire to get out of the house and meet like-minded people of the opposite sex. Or, it could be part of a decision to master the skills a paying employer desires.

What about taking a solitary walk in the woods? Here the drive to advance plays out as well. There are many possible reasons for wanting to hike. You might desire to get away from crowds, think freely, observe nature's beauty, listen to birds, or take in the healthful aspects of fresh air. All of these reasons for hiking are grounded in the drive to advance. In essence, what drives your decision to take the nature walk is the desire to feel better and improve your state of mind.

## THE DRIVE TO SERVE

While we can tie achievement with the drive to advance, catching the Spirit of Personal Economics will not come from the drive to advance alone. When employing the drive to advance, you must cultivate the drive to serve. In the drive to serve, you are being useful to others, which brings both pleasure and profit.

In fact, action in the drive to advance without the drive to serve can limit progress and self-respect. When you and others conduct yourselves in negative ways, you are usually acting solely in the drive to advance. You can easily recognize this behavior when it occurs. A motorist tails us on the highway, horn honking and headlights flashing.

Someone demands a faster exit from an airliner and shoves from behind. A patron in a restaurant fumes out loud to a hapless waiter over a dish served less than piping hot. A student cheats on a test painstakingly developed by their teacher. A high government official embezzles money from the state treasury.

In each of the above examples, the people lack the drive to serve. Each is considering his or her personal gain alone. If, instead, you act in a fashion that serves others, you will find a source of immense personal satisfaction. Personal reward comes from serving others, not merely from helping ourselves.

Basic to your life experiences, *everything you see in the world of products and services, and everything you receive from that world, result from actions taken by other people to serve and advance.* People have wanted to create the things that surround you. Whether newspapers, elevators, or antibiotics, somebody first wanted to serve the community and create these things.

On the island, your service in shelter-making helped lay the foundation for economic progress. As you served the community with your shelters, you also answered to your personal economic need – escaping basic hunger and pursuing your desire for extras. But the drive to serve goes deeper than work. It is important to your spiritual well-being.

You will often find that happy people offer something of value to other people. This could be a smile, a violin concerto, a good paint job, a successful homework assignment, or an improved toothbrush design.

In these examples, "offering something of value" is akin to creation. And in your creation of service for other people, you can find your sense of contribution to the community. Furthermore, because of this creation, others will appreciate you. *When you become useful and beneficial to the community, other people will recognize and praise your success.* And as others see you as successful, you will see yourself in the same way.

So what do you offer of value, and how do others show their appreciation? If you're a student, you satisfy your teacher with a well-executed term paper, and, as a result, you receive encouraging comments. If you're an artist, you turn mundane materials into things of beauty, and hundreds spend an afternoon at a museum to see your work. Even as a motorist, when you wave another motorist through at an intersection, you create a service someone else appreciates.

In the economy, those who capture the drive to serve will perform the job at hand to the best of their current ability. They also work in the belief that they have engaged in a useful task, well-worth their time and effort. In the drive to serve, no matter what your current ability, you have something to offer others in your community, something of value. All you have to do is recognize these valuable offerings and figure out a way for your offerings to benefit both you and others.

To do a job with the idea of getting it over with will not bring you fulfillment. It will not grant you the deeper, more satisfying economic well-being that comes when you act with the Spirit in mind. *In the world of self-improvement, a service provided with integrity, honesty, and sincerity will carry the day.*

## THE DRIVE TO EXCHANGE

We come now to the drive to exchange, the third motivational impulse for you to embrace. As a stepping stone to contentment in your personal economy, you must understand the drive to exchange: a natural and constructive tendency of people to engage in the act of giving or receiving one thing in return for another.

We constantly exchange things. Exchanges could involve work, time, ingenuity, a favor, or money in return for a needed object or service. These acts of exchange are at the heart of our behavior with other people. We base our communication with most of the people we meet on exchange, even if the exchange is in the non-money world. The following example illustrates this fact:

Let's say a friend invites you to a dinner party with several other people. The host of this party has reasons for inviting you to this occasion. One reason

could stem from a desire to see your reaction to a
newly prepared dish. Another could be the feeling
that your presence at the table would enhance the
atmosphere of the occasion. A third could be the
hope that your son and the host's daughter will
become better acquainted. Because of your personality, your taste in food, or your family, the host
wants you at this dinner event. If you deliver the
goods expected at the party, you have succeeded in
satisfying the needs of the host. You have provided
the service desired. As the creator of this service,
you have exported a non-money benefit to your host
on this occasion. In return, you have received an
enjoyable evening.

Now, let's look at the money world. Here, you
offer your work, time, skills, and production in exchange for money or goods. You export, or offer, your
skills or products to others – a government, clients,
or a business that employs you. Your desire to gain
purchasing power, the power to buy material goods
or services, drives your efforts to exchange.

On the island, the trading of goods and services

allowed you and the islanders to divide up work according to your specialties. As consumption on the island became more complex, exchange by barter gave way to money-based exchange. Money then became the lubricant of the exchange process. Once money entered the community, getting money became the goal, for the possession of money measured one's ability to pay for goods. It measured one's ability to exchange.

You must understand another aspect of the drive to exchange. It also reflects our deep-seated ideal of fairness in human relations. As we interact with each other, we naturally strive to achieve fairness in exchange. In the act of exchange, a substitution occurs in which two things of agreed-upon, equal value are traded – money for bread, money for work, bread for work, or a favor for a favor. Just like on the island, where one shelter first exchanged for one blanket and then increased to four blankets, *as perceived values change for a certain item, so do the proportions of the exchange*. Generally, the exchange value of a piece of work will rise if many people or businesses demand the work, if the work is of a high quality, or if the work cannot be easily replaced.

Values in exchange constantly change. A newcomer on a job earns minimum wage. After five years of experience and consistent effort at self-improvement in the workplace, the seasoned worker receives several times his or her old pay. If suddenly, all professional football teams want to hire the same quarterback, the price tag for this player's skills skyrockets overnight. Managers and workers in a company pull together to increase the quality, uniqueness, and popularity of its product. Then, the total value of the company rises as investors pay additional money for shares of the company.

Keep in mind that, in exchange, whether it's money for work, or products and services for money, the equality in values remains. For example, let's say a home-seller insists on $200,000 for the sale of a house when no one offers more than $175,000. The property does not exchange hands, and, in a practical sense, the house is worthless. Only when the seller lowers the sales price or when the buyer raises the offer price can the values equalize. Only then can an exchange happen.

On the island, you exchanged time and effort for food and clothing. In today's diverse economy, it works the same way. As you improve your skills in the drive to advance, you will find people ready to exchange money for your useful service. You need only be productive, useful, and of service to other people. The quality of your service, as well as its usefulness to others, will determine the price you get paid for what you do.

## THE POWER OF SYNERGY (COOPERATION)

Our desire for recognition, respect, and reward for our spent time and effort runs deep. Most people want to increase the perceived value of their work or product – a normal, healthy practice. Action in the drives to advance, serve, and exchange answers this innate need. In your drive to advance you will drive to serve and this will make your drive to exchange all the more successful. It is the synergy of these three drives deep within you that propels you to economic success.

The important lesson here is that when you act in the Spirit of Personal Economics, action in the drive to advance is for the benefit of others, not for your own selfishness. The drive to advance works

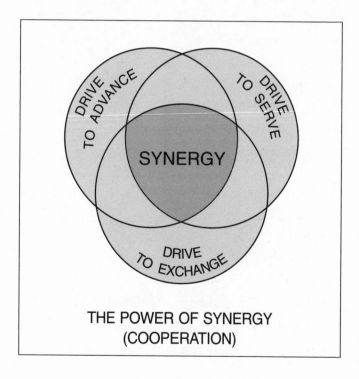

THE POWER OF SYNERGY
(COOPERATION)

with the drive to serve, and together, they enrich the drive to exchange. Remember, action in one of the three drives alone will not bring you economic well-being.

As you do the activities on the next page, remember what you've learned:

* When we act in a fashion that serves others, we find a source of immense personal satisfaction.

* One person's gain can also provide satisfaction to others.

* Unless your efforts somehow benefit others, no one will recognize them.

* In the world of self-improvement, a service provided with integrity, honesty, and effort will carry the day.

* The drive to exchange is a natural tendency in people to engage in the act of giving or taking one thing in return for another.

* Your desire to gain purchasing power, the power

to buy any material good or service, drives your
efforts to serve and exchange.

## ACTIVITIES

➡ LOOK AT HOW YOU USE THE DRIVES TO ADVANCE,
SERVE, AND EXCHANGE. THINK OF A GOAL YOU HAVE
ACHIEVED, SUCH AS SUCCESSFULLY GOING TO A MALL
AND PURCHASING A PAIR OF SHOES. HOW DID THESE
THREE DRIVES HELP YOU TO REACH THAT GOAL?
DID YOUR DRIVE TO ADVANCE MOTIVATE YOU TO
OBTAIN A NEW STYLE OF SHOES? HOW DID YOU
USE YOUR DRIVE TO SERVE TO OBTAIN THE MONEY
FOR THE SHOES? WHAT DID YOU EXCHANGE (TIME,
FAVORS, WORK, MONEY?) IN ORDER TO BE ABLE TO
BUY THE SHOES?

➡ THINK OF A GOAL YOU HAVE YET TO ACHIEVE, LIKE
BUYING A NEW HOUSE, GOING TO COLLEGE, OR AT-
TENDING A CONCERT. HOW MIGHT THE DRIVES TO
ADVANCE, SERVE, AND EXCHANGE HELP YOU REACH
THIS GOAL? WHAT CAN YOU DO TO MAKE YOUR
QUEST EASIER? HOW CAN YOU USE OTHERS' DRIVES

TO ADVANCE, SERVE, AND EXCHANGE TO HELP YOU
REACH YOUR GOAL? CAN YOU IMAGINE SOMEONE
WILLING TO OFFER YOU HELP BECAUSE IT HELPS
THEM, TOO?

## MAKING A VIRTUE OF YOUR WORK

When viewing your options in the economy,
consider yourself an independent, thinking being.
After all, how you view your economic potential
links to how you view yourself. The choice is yours.
You may believe that your physical body and mental
state are such that it would be a folly to aspire to
become an eight-hour-a-day figure skater or a bas-
ketball player earning millions of dollars in salary,
but you can take stock of where you are today.

## ACTIVITY

➡ ASK YOURSELF, "HOW CAN I IMPROVE WHAT I AM
DOING RIGHT NOW? WHAT DO PEOPLE REALLY WANT
THAT I CAN PROVIDE OR LEARN TO PROVIDE?" WHY

NOT TAKE A FEW MINUTES TO WRITE DOWN YOUR
ANSWERS?

Many people out there ask questions like these,
act upon their answers, and improve their well-
being.

Let's take all of this to a practical level. Your
economic options boil down to the following:

❉ Should I work or kick back?

❉ Should I use up my time and resources investing in myself, or should I keep my abilities,
skills, and attitudes fixed in place?

❉ Should I go through life striving to produce and
consume, nurturing my drives to advance, serve,
and exchange? Or should I reject my pursuit of
prosperity in this context and work outside
social norms?

Your response to these three questions will
determine your material and mental well-being
throughout your life. But realize up front that those

who benefit from the Spirit of Personal Economics Philosophy choose:

❧ Work.

❧ Investment in the self.

❧ Action within society.

You could become one of the people who supports a rising standard of living for millions.

## TO WORK OR NOT TO WORK

You can choose to work or not to work. Most likely, you have chosen to work or are searching for a job. But, let's say you have decided to work as little as possible. Consider this example:

Let's say that your goal is to spend as much time as possible relaxing in cafés, drinking coffee, and eating cake, while the workaday world toils on, fighting traffic congestion, handling the performance evaluations of bosses, and dealing with incessant bills in the mail.

In fact, you have to work rather hard to live by this decision. Unless you are of independent means, your café existence will force you to learn how to make do with the bare minimum from the material world. This takes work. Having to economize your food or clothing expenditures takes effort. Walking to your café, when you would rather take a bus or taxi, takes work.

It goes deeper than this. As you pass the day away, sipping your beverages, your mind will tell you that you are wasting time without creating anything. Called psychological entropy, you might feel it as estrangement, depression, a non-directional state of mind, or quite simply, boredom. More importantly, unless you have a tremendous capacity for profound self-esteem to fall back on, your café existence will not bring you happiness. The reason for this is not complicated.

Deep down, everyone desires to be acknowledged. Most people want to partake in creating things that others can appreciate, a statement that rings true even for the 17th century Swiss philosopher Jean-Jacques Rousseau. Here was a man who removed himself from society, turning the solitary existence into an art form, yet spent most of his adult life in constant worry. The reason for this anxiety was simple enough. Rousseau worried that readers in Paris and Geneva would not appreciate his writings. Solitary by choice, Rousseau still craved acceptance by people in the outside world.

If you sip coffee in the café, the world of luxury cars, compact discs, Irish step dancing, stock market speculation, and new Häagen-Dazs flavors will only serve to alienate you, since, as a coffee-sipper, you have no means with which to obtain anything.

You might be thinking, "Doesn't everyone want to relax in cafés? After all, café-sitting is a perfectly natural and desirable use of time." However, for the vast majority of people sitting in cafés, the enjoyment of ambience serves as a respite from work, as an earned activity, not as a flight from humanity.

By working, you help make the economy function. In the economy, you find that your sense of well-being comes from employment in useful endeavors. Work is the motor that propels the economy, and you and others use the drives to advance, serve, and exchange to create value. You create materials of value so that those materials have lasting imprints on the world. In them, you find the basis for your existence. You, as others do, have the universal need to work and the desire to express yourself.

More so, you depend upon the work of others. The following example illustrates this point:

Let us say that you have just inherited ten million dollars. You desire now to take advantage of this exhilarating situation by ceasing all forms of work. You place your ten million dollars in a regular bank savings account where it earns 3 percent annual interest. You do not concern yourself with investment strategies, and you have no cares about the safety of your deposit, since you have placed your money in one of the world's largest and best-managed banks. Your annual payments from the bank will be 3 percent of ten million dollars, or $300,000. This comes to a monthly income of $25,000.

Yet this monthly payment from your bank would not be available to you were it not for the countless interactions of thousands, if not millions of people, all involved with planning, working, and creating value for themselves and for others. Your interest payment comes from the money your bank receives from the companies and individuals with whom the bank does business. Each of these companies and individuals receives payments from their business associates. In the end, there are millions of people contributing to your bank, which has enabled it to send you a monthly check.

In this example, you may not see yourself as having to work, but where would you be without the work of others? At some point in time, someone had to earn the ten million dollars you inherited. Even living on the inheritance, you still must see yourself as integrated into, and completely dependent upon, the world of work.

What you produce and consume plugs you into a relationship with the whole economy. Later, when we discuss the role of occupations and professions, you will see the importance of this relationship. For now, recognize the depth of your connection to others as they work and consume. *Everyone depends on everyone else.* Because we are all so interconnected, you must not consider some forms of work as more prestigious or as more noble than others. With this understanding, the company manager, the doctor, and the dishwasher in the corner café can feel the same sense of pride over a job well done because both provide and contribute to the economy.

Everyone's work connects to the heart of the economy and to your own. You will fully depend on the provision of service by others at every step of your economic journey through life. Whether you struggle to purchase your first house or idly contemplate an addition to a collection of rare writing instruments, you connect with everyone's work. After all, fountain pen collectors must give due respect to the work behind fountain pen designs.

Imagine what would happen if the dishwasher at a local restaurant quit. If you go to that restaurant, perhaps you will have to wait an extra half-hour for food because a prep cook, a manager, or a waitress has to cover the job of washing dishes in addition to their normal workload.

## ACTIVITY

➠ GO TO A RESTAURANT. THINK OF ALL THE PEOPLE NECESSARY TO MAKE THE RESTAURANT RUN SMOOTH- LY. TAKE OUT A SHEET OF PAPER AND DRAW THE WEB SHOWN ON THE NEXT PAGE. LIST EACH JOB IN A BUBBLE (WAITRESS, BUSBOY, ETC.). THEN, DRAW CONNECTING LINES FROM THAT EMPLOYEE TO EVERY- ONE WHOM THAT EMPLOYEE DEPENDS UPON. THE OWNER HAS BEEN PLACED IN THE MIDDLE BECAUSE THE SUCCESS OF HIS OR HER RESTAURANT DEPENDS ENTIRELY UPON THE STAFF AT THE RESTAURANT. THE MAIN POINT: WE ARE ALL INTERCONNECTED.

One of the greatest advantages of respecting all human effort is the peace of mind it brings, a peace of mind that comes from the knowledge that we are here together, and together we live out our destinies.

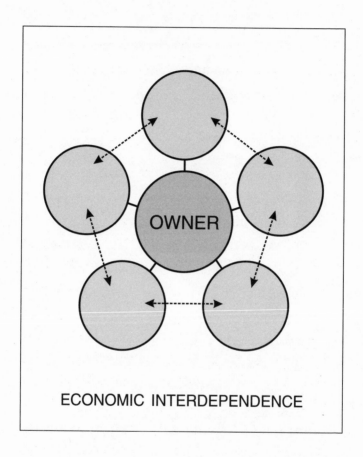

ECONOMIC INTERDEPENDENCE

This peace of mind can lead you to a bigger sense of respect for diversity. Love of the economic efforts of your fellow men and women as they search for economic success can help you find your own sense of well-being. It reinforces a greater respect for the production and consumption that surrounds us all.

## To Invest In Yourself
## or Not

The second choice you must make with respect to your work is whether or not you will invest in yourself, whether or not you will increase the value of your work. When you invest in yourself, you participate in the process of continuous learning and improvement.

Self-investment will route you to greater accomplishments and personal productivity, and solidify your connection to the way of thinking that brings deep economic satisfaction.

How do we most commonly invest in ourselves? We invest in ourselves first by embracing the virtues embodied in our cultures, such as honesty, integrity, loyalty, dependability, and friendship. We invest in ourselves by learning as much as possible about how the human world functions. In particular, this means that we must try to understand how we can pursue our dreams in concert with the people in our community. We invest in ourselves by improving ourselves in body and mind and by learning how to serve others through acquired skills.

Later, in Chapter 5, you will see in detail how investment in yourself, a vigorous act of personal growth, propels your economic opportunity and pro- ductivity forward.

## WORKING FROM WITHIN OR RAGING FROM WITHOUT

How do you view yourself in the community? How do you view your worth and economic accom- plishment? If you accept that you have the potential to contribute to the economy, and that others can offer valuable resources to help you along your way, then you anchor yourself on a path toward economic well-being. *An important source of happiness comes from a feeling of belonging to this world.* Our com- munity extends far beyond family and work asso- ciates. Feeling a bond with your larger community can be a great source of personal serenity. Each individual, part of the larger community, desires economic success at some level and lives according to their own uniqueness as a thinking, planning, and advance-oriented person. As you live out your life, you will profit from the diversity of the people you meet. This diversity is most apparent in the many activities of producers and consumers in your community.

In fact, the products you use can define you; they define how you fit within your community. Whole social groupings often connect through common tastes in consumption. Certain groups are into pickup trucks, country music, hot dogs, and beer. Others may prefer titanium bicycles, organic fruit smoothies, silent stunt kites, and books with color photographs of natural landscapes. Often, these consumption items become displays of identity for each group, and each group will fiercely defend its right to consume them. And you should respond to this great diversity of desires with your usefulness, productivity, and service.

As we work to improve ourselves, we must work within society. In society, we gain our recognition, praise, and rewards. Those who search for consolation outside of the human environment will likely reinforce their feelings of alienation, raising the possibility of their acting out in inhumane, non-ethical ways.

Your attitude is crucial. If you choose to feel exploited by your employer, elected officials, insurance broker, or by the world at large, you set yourself up for a negative mental attitude that can push you away from personal economic well-being. But, if you decisively accept that getting ahead in the world means proffering useful ideas that you can translate into appreciated results, you will not feel exploited, and you will be rewarded in proportion to your contribution. Complainers who offer no constructive or helpful solutions are seldom rewarded. If you do complain, be certain to add your thoughtful remedy; be aware of the world and be ready to help. You will be amazed at the changes in your life and at the reactions in those with whom you come in contact.

So how do we go about learning to offer solutions instead of emphasizing the problem?

## Activity

- ➡ Spend a day noticing when anyone complains. When they do, try to think of a great solution for them. If you start to complain, immediately sort through the reasons for your complaint and then begin to think of solutions to your problem. The faster you become solution-oriented, the faster you can overcome each challenge and gain control of your personal economic well-being.

Working both within and for your community will benefit you tremendously.

Remember:

- An important source of happiness comes from a feeling of belonging to this world.
- The products you use define you and your niche

in the community.

❧ As you work to improve yourself, you will gain greater economic well-being and contentment, as long as you work within society.

## THE SPIRIT OF PERSONAL ECONOMICS CHECKLIST

There is an immense payoff if you:

✓ Pursue your goals.

✓ Adopt and express a positive mental attitude.

✓ Utilize the drives to advance, serve, and exchange.

✓ Work and contribute.

✓ Invest in yourself.

✓ Work within your community and allow others to help you.

When you accomplish these key elements, you will have taken the steps toward your personal economic success and contentment – the foundation of the Spirit of Personal Economics. You may then choose to live as a minimalist and consume a single loaf of bread per day, sleep in a simple hut, and spend your days meditating on the meaning of life. But at least you have chosen to do so. Then, you can look on with equanimity while much of humankind consumes luxury cars, perfume, sausages, dark beer, and Southern European vacations.

## WHAT'S NEXT

Now that you have learned the basics of how an economy functions and the attitude that will help you navigate through the economy, let's go on to discover how to enjoy your new way of thinking about your personal economics. In Part Two, you will learn fun ways to enjoy your new perspective as a consumer, self-investor, and seller of your skills and services.

# Part Two

## Enjoying the Spirit of Personal Economics

# 4

## A New Way to Look
## at Your Consumption

WHAT GOOD IS GAINING ECONOMIC SUCCESS if you don't enjoy it? In the chapters that follow, you will learn how to take pleasure from your actions as you combine your accomplishments with a purposeful connection to your community. Also, you will learn how to look at the meaningful impacts the material world makes on our lives.

We begin with your consumption and use of

things. Through your own spending decisions, you can gain an appreciation of your connections with the world and an appreciation of the people your consumption supports. Here, you will learn how to enjoy your economic choices to the fullest.

## WHAT WE CONSUME MAKES THE WORLD GO 'ROUND

With a few thousand years of developed traditions, consumption has evolved into a common behavior that distinguishes people from animals. We are the only creatures on the planet that consciously make and acquire a multitude of things in order to use them and, as our cultures have evolved, the only creatures to consume beyond answering the need for physical survival. We are the only creatures who have linked consumption with self-esteem, diversion, and achievement.

We do not consume by accident. We do not consume because we lack imagination concerning what to do with ourselves. We make a conscious choice to consume, and this modern-day choice involves far more than an effort in self-indulgence. Consumption can be an act of sublime privacy. It can express one's individuality. It can reflect our personal tastes – who we are – just as it defines social groupings like the bike lovers or the beer drinkers.

For example, if you choose to buy a particular music CD, you are asserting your character. You are saying in essence, "This is my choice of music. This is what I like. This is how I choose to spend my money. I may be influenced by the views of my friends, advertisers, and magazine writers, but so what? I expect pleasure from consuming this kind of music, for I believe it will resonate with who I am."

Does it really matter how you are influenced, if, when you buy a product or service, you come away with a feeling of satisfaction? *What really matters is that you enjoy and benefit from the products and services you have acquired. What matters is that you recognize that when you use your buying power (ability to pay), you are supporting an entire web of people just like you.*

If you order a hamburger at a restaurant, you

say, knowingly or not, "This is now my hamburger. I have chosen this food as my sustenance. By eating this hamburger, I will unite with the productive forces of this restaurant and with all the farmers, butchers, bankers, and trades people who made this moment possible." Conversely, if you boycott or refuse to buy the hamburger, you are saying, "I will not unite with these productive forces." In this way, your buying power may even be used to create social change.

Your desire to consume and your persistent efforts to act on this desire provide the incentives for others to act as producers who will work in pursuit of their *own* economic prosperity. At the same time, producers usually buy other materials necessary to make what you purchase – materials ranging from accounting services to legal advice, marketing expertise to machines and buildings. And the people who produce these things will buy even more goods and services from other suppliers. For example, the accountant will need computers, pads, and pencils in order to provide accounting advice. All through this process, which continues in a long, unending chain, these acts of producing, buying, and selling bring millions of consumer goods to the marketplace and provide millions of people their livelihoods.

Our drive to acquire and use things stimulates those around us to create objects that can be sold. Our desire to profit from the tastes of the community motivates more production and innovation.

So how can you enjoy your own consumption more fully? How can your awareness of others help you?

Remember:

≈ Your consumption expresses your individuality and reflects who you are. Feel good when you buy that CD. Not only will it bring you hours of listening pleasure, but also, you will have supported the people who created, produced, and distributed it.

≈ Your use of goods and services can give you a sense of security and economic well-being.

❧ To acquire is a natural human state.

❧ Your consumption helps the community by furthering economic growth.

## ENJOYING TECHNOLOGY

The special, ever-changing methods we use to put things together, called technology, sustain the economy.

Today, people toss around the concept of "technology" with surprising ease. Look in the newspaper, listen to the radio, and eventually, you'll hear a couple of common phrases: "We live in a technological age," and "High-tech is where the action is." Sometimes, people view technology with a suspicious eye, as though new contraptions, machines, and methodologies are unnatural and sinister.

Actually, just the opposite is true. Technology is a natural occurrence that works with, and is an expression of, the synergy of our drives to advance, serve, and exchange. It has been with us since the dawn of humanity. Technology is not only comprised of computers and microchips, it's also the methods we use to make a product or service and the manner in which machines, equipment, people, skills, and management mix together to form a product. *Everything we consume involves technology.*

For example, the technology of elementary spear-making might call for a mix of dexterous hands, sturdy branches, flint, and cord to connect the rock spearhead to the branch. Advanced spear-building could call for a technology that mixes machine tools and computers. The machine tools would mold and straighten steel spear shafts. The computers would measure the exact length, thickness, and impact strength of the steel in the shafts. *In short, technology is how people make things and perform their work.*

Once again, the island economy simplifies the point. The islanders shared a common drive to produce things in the most efficient and inexpensive way. An entrepreneurial spirit drove them into their different work activities. Always, some islander would invent a new technology to bring cheaper and higher quality products to the island.

On the island, you used creativity to make more comfortable, useful shelters. Eventually, islanders chose from an array of efficiently built and competitively-priced dwellings.

The drive to invent new technology remains with us today. Virtually all products begin with a unique technology that improves as time moves on. With the passing of time and the accumulation of knowledge, technologies respond to the desire for the new and improved.

Thus, the technology behind many homes today involves complicated electrical networks, plumbing, construction materials, fabric, and design that have their origins in the Neolithic age. Technology, as you can see, has developed as people have worked to better their lives.

You may be asking, "Why is the history of technology so important?" Well, if you know that technology began with a common drive to improve our economic well-being, that knowledge can help you appreciate the inventiveness of past technologies as they shaped the world of goods and services. Past technologies make today's technologies possible. When you consume products and services, you can now see yourself as part of a community in the present and also as part of a long chain of inventive, creative people.

Remember:

🔥 Technologies are how people make things and perform their work.

🔥 Technologies always evolve and change, building on past experience and the accumulation of knowledge and wisdom.

🔥 Technology is a natural occurrence that works with, and is an expression of, the synergy of our drives to advance, serve, and exchange.

🔥 New technologies bring us improved and more useful products to consume.

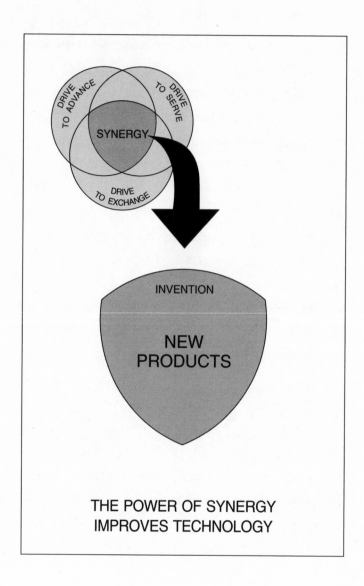

## A DEEPER VIEW
## OF OUR URGE TO CONSUME

Is the act of consumption an escape? Is the desire for a larger home, a more powerful car, or the excitement of an action movie a turn away from something more substantive and meaningful?

Yes, consumption can be an escape, but not from a more meaningful, deeper life. In your consumption of essentials, you escape death and starvation and an ennui that would irrepressibly set in if you did not consume.

How do you occupy yourself much of the time? You consume. When you consume products, whether they be basic to your survival, to help you in your work, or for your entertainment, you connect with the world, with the makers of your acquired items, and with the store or business that sells those items. You also spend your hard-earned money when you consume, money earned from a job that allows you to contribute to your community. When your desires play out in the economy, either as a consumer or a producer, you accomplish something very worthwhile.

Consumption can also be a celebration. Your conscious desire to validate your services to others or to reap the harvest of your self-investments drives much of your consumption. Consumption is your due reward. *Most acts of consumption have degrees of escape and degrees of celebration in them.*

As a lone islander, you found that the consumption of shelter could come only after searching for materials. Living in the shelter became a due reward for effort expended, a celebration of this effort. With the growth of the community, you decided to acquire a hammock. In all likelihood, you used the hammock for the purpose of relaxation or daydreaming, and in this sense, consumption was an escape.

Philosophers have written that art and science are the greatest forms of escape that humankind has developed. Think of the technology of the luxury car, a honed fusion of art and science brought forth through years of invention. Not only can we escape by buying and using a luxury car, we can also escape by designing and building it.

And just like the luxury car, all products and services are a mixture of the aesthetic and the practical, of art and science, and all are forms of escape.

It is legitimate to regard products with the same awe we accord to art and science. After all, inspiration for some of today's laptop computers comes from Leonardo da Vinci's drawings. Many styles of toothpaste tubes are marvels of engineering. Breakfast cereals cater to every possible health need. The technology of production is applied art and science.

In a most basic form of escape, a person suffering from hunger consumes food. Another form of escape comes to those who can choose a first class seat on a transatlantic flight. The pleasure of having a wide seat, rather than a narrow seat for eight hours, outweighs the pain of spending more money. Both forms of consumption are normal and natural, following the inclination to improve and enjoy life on a daily basis.

You have seen that our drive to create diverse goods and services fuels the economy. This does not mean you will feel a constant urge to increase your level of consumption, although most people do, if only at an elementary level. A child, out of the running for a luxury car, may still appreciate the variety of chewing gum available at the supermarket checkout counter.

The growth and diversity of goods and services does not come from a conspiracy of a cloistered few, but rather from the expression of what we want at a deep psychological and physiological level. These wants align with our drive to better our lives.

So what are we left with? We have the soda bottle in six sizes and a particular brand of toothpaste in at least ten varieties. Espresso cafés serve more than cappuccino in a cup. You can also have your cappuccino in small, medium, and large; hot, iced, or blended; with one, two, or three shots of espresso; with non-fat, low-fat, whole, or soy milk; with whipped cream or without; decaffeinated or caffeinated.

And do you know what? We love it!

As you set about gaining more satisfaction from each product or service you consume, think about the following:

- ۞ Consumption is a sought escape from the threat of deprivation and from daily routines that can make your life dull.

- ۞ Your consumption is a celebration of your due reward.

- ۞ Your consumption is your expressed appreciation of a product that combines art and science in a way that satisfies your deepest psychological and physical needs.

Be honest with yourself as you face the vast array of consumable goods. Gaining deeper economic well-being will depend upon your ability to appreciate your own personal consumption.

## ACTIVITIES

➡ THINK ABOUT WHAT YOU HAVE RECENTLY BOUGHT FOR YOURSELF. HOW DID YOU FEEL WHEN YOU BOUGHT YOUR ITEM? WHAT DESIRE OR NEED REQUIRED YOU TO PURCHASE THAT ITEM?

➥ Hopefully, you felt satisfied and pleased with your purchase. After all, you've had a chance to celebrate your own hard work with a reward. You've had a chance for escape. You've had a chance to express your appreciation for that product with your money. Think about your purchase again. Write a list of all the people that your item has helped, including all suppliers and manufacturers.

Your purchases have supported the livelihoods of many people. As long as you're considering your choices wisely and trying to support others as you help yourself, you're on the right track!

## The Spirit of Personal Economics Checklist

✓ You have begun to enjoy the way your consumption connects you with others.

✓ You appreciate the fact that people consume to express their individuality, to improve their well-being, to entertain, to celebrate, and to escape.

✓ You know that what you have consumed gave someone else pleasure to make and sell.

✓ You understand that through new technologies, people improve the products and services they sell.

## WHAT'S NEXT?

If you strive to be a big consumer and long to cast a wide net over the fruits of this world, you will have to earn the ability to pay. Don't despair if this is your goal, and you still feel you have a long way to go. In the next chapters, you will find ways to increase your personal productivity and improve your personal economic well-being.

# 5

## INVEST IN YOURSELF

So how do you increase your personal productivity and enjoy the process? How do you increase your economic well-being? Simple – invest!

The very sound of the word conjures up images of finance. Usually, you see investment as a complex business activity involving financial companies. When making personal decisions, you might think of investment as the purchase of stocks, bonds, or some other financial asset. Often, homeowners look upon their homes as investments with the hope that the value of their home will increase.

In fact, you can view investment as a very simple concept. *Investment is the time taken with calculation to improve the future.* To invest your time in a project, you take that time to accomplish a task that will bear fruit. You allocate this time with the conviction that you will not waste your efforts, that you will gain an advantage from your activity, and that you will create tools conducive to reaching your goal. *At the heart of all your investments are your positive expectations.*

From the perspective of your personal economics, think of investment as all forms of money and time spent by the government, companies, and most importantly, you, in order to gain skills, tools, and products to enhance future well-being.

When your government spends money on highways, immunization programs, schools, and facilities that dispose of nuclear waste, the government invests in the well-being of the community. When a business enterprise upgrades existing floor space or adds new computers to its production processes, the firm invests in its future. When you choose to spend time learning marketing, a new language, or body-building, you invest in yourself.

All of these investments will create the foundation of your economic well-being. All these investments increase your ability to be productive in making and offering goods and services to the rest of the economy.

## TIME, INVESTMENT, AND PERSONAL ECONOMIC GROWTH

We return to the notion of time, because how you enjoy the Spirit of Personal Economics will depend on how you spend your time. When it comes to investment, your use of time becomes critical.

The time people have taken to improve the future has allowed them to build shelters, produce food, fight disease, and establish global communications systems. This ability to invest in the future has allowed the human race to satisfy its voracious desire for economic growth.

Another "fact of nature": investments take time

to bear fruit. In light of this, how extraordinary it is that for the past 3000 years or more, we have consciously chosen to sacrifice present consumption, even if just for a moment, in order to build a better tomorrow.

For you, our islander, the issue of needed shelter against the elements quickly created the necessity for investment. Perhaps for the first few nights, collected branches served as shelter. After that, the urge for more permanent, safe lodgings compelled you to hack out a cave or to cut wood in order to build four walls and a roof.

The collection of branches was a form of sufficient shelter investment for the first night or two. The decisions and actions necessary to build the four-walled shelter involved a more time-intensive form of investment. In the latter case, you took the time normally used for gathering food to construct the shelter. This investment paid off. Once completed, you used your experience in investment to think of ways to improve food gathering from within the relative security of a water-resistant home.

When the island became populated and the islanders specialized in certain lines of work, the issue of investment remained. Many shelter-makers felt compelled to distinguish themselves in shelter building. Strategies included steps to find tools, space, and time for the building of better shelters. These steps were investments. The builders who fashioned their own tools invested their time to prepare for future production. In a sense, when you invest, you are saving, and this saving becomes the alternative to consumption.

If you suddenly strike it rich, earn an income, or turn a business profit, you must decide whether to consume or invest. Perhaps you will spend most of the money consuming. But you might also decide that a part of this money should be pooled and saved for future use.

You might plan to invest in an education, expecting that what you will learn will benefit you in the future. Or you might decide to save based on a feeling of uncertainty. You and your business might save funds, expecting to invest in the development of new, competitive technologies.

The desire to save a portion of your income is a universal economic urge, akin to consumption itself. But no matter what, we strive to obtain the freedom to consume whenever we want, and saving helps us achieve that freedom.

When you choose to invest in your future, you take the time to improve it. You do this even if it means saving now and forgoing present activities of consumption. Nonetheless, your investments solidify a happier economic future. Your investments increase your ability to be productive, useful, and of service. They increase the options you have for a pleasing economic lifestyle. And the act of investment that pays you consistently is investment in yourself.

## ACTIVITY

➡ TAKE THE TIME TO OBSERVE PEOPLE WITH A SYMPATHETIC EYE. HOW ARE THEY SIMILAR TO YOU? LOOK AT THE WAITRESS WHO SERVES YOU, THE GAS STATION ATTENDANT, THE CORPORATE EXEC-

UTIVE. DO YOU THINK THESE PEOPLE HAVE THE
SAME INVESTMENT DESIRES AS YOU? HOW ARE THEY
SIMILAR TO YOU IN THEIR DECISIONS TO INVEST IN
THEMSELVES? HOW ARE THEY DIFFERENT?

So how can you invest in yourself and boost
your productivity?

## INVEST IN YOUR BODY

First, you must invest in your body. To do this,
you must accept that your body is a marvelous,
natural machine that can be directed by your mind.
This machine thrives on food, exercise, and a re-
laxed spirit.

We need our health. There is nothing new in
this idea. We have been investing our time for
millennia to deal with the issue of physical vigor
and disease prevention. It's up to you to take advantage of this legacy. Since you have the power to
decide how you pass your time and how you use the
products of this world, you have an obligation to
choose well when it comes to investment in your

physical well-being.

Concern for your health does not place a mandatory prohibition on fatty foods, alcohol, nicotine, and long periods of time in front of a television. Yet, it does require a conscious effort to understand the effects of certain products on the physical body and to use current information for safe and healthy behavior.

The feeling of healthful energy is delightful. In addition, the sound, physical body enhances a sensation of social well-being, since most people have a mental picture of what makes the human figure desirable. Over several thousand years, cultures have depicted an ideal for the human form. Often, this ideal is strong and shapely. The "hard body" is neither an invention of Hollywood screenwriters nor of personal fitness trainers. If you were to visit the ancient village of Delphi in Greece, you would see clear evidence that, 2000 years ago, the ideal male and female had vigorous bodies.

It's up to you. Your deep yearning for physical perfection can contribute to your happiness. Of course, it goes without saying that not everyone has the body-type or metabolism conducive to becoming the "ideal." Nevertheless, you can strive to develop your unique physical characteristics to the fullest. For example, everyone thrives on exercise. The means for developing physical fitness are everywhere, from parks and walking trails to fitness clubs with organized classes.

So how do you go about respecting your body?

## ACTIVITY

➡ DECIDE TO EXERCISE EVERY DAY FOR A WEEK. EAT VEGETABLES AND FRUITS EACH DAY WITH YOUR REGULAR MEALS. IN THIS WEEK, AVOID NEGATIVE THOUGHTS CONCERNING YOUR BODY. WHEN YOU DO FEEL BAD, FIND TIME TO TAKE A WALK. GO TO THE GYM. EXERCISE. RECORD HOW MUCH BETTER YOU FEEL WHEN YOU TAKE TIME TO INVEST IN YOUR BODY BY EXERCISING, EATING RIGHT, AND THINKING POSITIVELY.

A sound, physical body feeds self-respect. This

self-respect prepares you for the most important investment of all:

## INVESTMENT IN
## YOUR MIND

Education determines your economic destiny. Through education, you learn skills that command a value in the eyes of others. You learn the wonderful feeling that comes from being knowledgeable. With education, you piggyback on the accumulated knowledge and wisdom of the ages. You learn that as human history has progressed, people have worked collectively to better the lives of millions through learning and experience.

When you occupy yourself with education, you invest in yourself for a better economic future. But getting an education takes time. It takes effort. It takes money. Despite its cost, you must seek education.

It is possible to be self-educated. You can aim to teach yourself a skill worthy of an income. However, in the collective drive to advance, almost all communities have developed institutions that teach skills in a group setting. In groups, we have an instant base of comparison for our efforts, and we often receive inspiration from others who excel. The extensive educational systems of modern society are waiting to be mined by the ambitious. All you need is an educational goal in sight, the desire to reach it, and the persistence to follow through with effort.

When you invest in both your body and your mind, you take the vital steps necessary to gain and maintain the economic success you desire. The diagram on the next page demonstrates the continuous learning loop: more investment in your body and mind increases your learning, which will increase your productivity, which will make you want to invest even more, and so on.

## ACTIVITIES

➡ THINK OF WHAT YOU WANT TO LEARN THE MOST, PERHAPS RELATED TO YOUR BUSINESS OR YOUR PERSONAL GOALS. MAKE A LIST OF YOUR EDUCATIONAL GOALS.

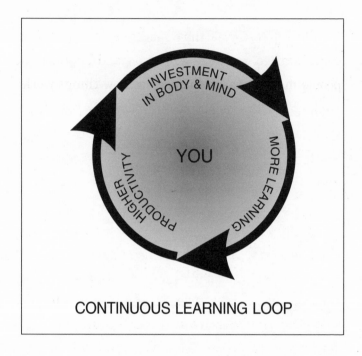

**CONTINUOUS LEARNING LOOP**

➡ TAKE THE TIME TODAY TO LEARN A LITTLE MORE ABOUT THOSE SUBJECTS. IF YOU WANT TO GO TO COLLEGE OR CONTINUE YOUR EDUCATION, CHECK OUT COMMUNITY AND FOUR-YEAR COLLEGES TODAY. GO ONLINE. BORROW A BOOK FROM THE LIBRARY. DO SOMETHING TO PURSUE YOUR INVESTMENT IN YOUR MIND.

The technologies that have built our material world started with the education and efforts that people made to teach themselves how things work. Walking on the moon, saving domestic pets from infection, and enjoying Häagen-Dazs ice creams would not be possible unless thousands of people took the time to invest in their futures.

## YOUR INVESTMENTS IN YOURSELF CREATE OUR OCCUPATIONS AND PROFESSIONS

When you make investments in yourself, you profit from the massive knowledge stored by those who came before you. You benefit from past efforts to produce goods and services. Your investments in yourself are your personal efforts to join this process.

Say you desire to work in a profession you find challenging. You also want to contribute directly to the welfare of others. You choose to become a heart surgeon. In order for this dream to become a reality, you must invest in yourself, business enterprises must invest in themselves, and the government must invest in the community at large.

You will invest time, energy, and money to learn the trade of heart surgery to the satisfaction of yourself, your teachers, the profession, and your patients. But you will find this investment impossible unless you take advantage of the results of past investments made by people who developed your trade: surgical instruments, medicines, textbooks, college courses, and government and professional guidelines for the practice of heart surgery.

All the materials in the community that give you the opportunity to become a heart surgeon have been refined over centuries. During this time, people have made decisions to invest in the future by accumulating knowledge and improving technologies. These investments provide the foundation from which you propel yourself into the heart surgery profession.

Once in the profession, you earn an income by providing a service others perceive as important. You will be paid in direct proportion to the quality and relative availability of your service. In this example, your income will be quite high. You have earned your personal economic success by investing in yourself and building on the investments of others.

Should you use your professional skills to invent and market new instruments that improve heart health overall, your past investments will again pay off by allowing you to enter the market for medical equipment. You may start a company that employs many people and sells its products at home and abroad. You would be a part of the economic growth process.

The same goes for any other profession you can think of. The airplane mechanic, the math teacher, the automobile designer, the tax lawyer, the sports newscaster, the advertising copywriter, the cellist, and the banker all perform useful services that require education. All depend upon developed products and the investments of people who have come before them. Individuals, investing in themselves to improve their skills, sustain the prosperity and opportunities in the economy.

Investing in yourself connects you with the community, and your investment becomes the fuel that nourishes your journey toward personal economic fulfillment.

## WHAT TO DO
## ABOUT PESSIMISM

If an economy passes through a several-year period of decline, only to continue its upward trajectory, how can the same people, once depressed about economic conditions, become upbeat again? The answer lies in expectations.

If you expect failure, then failure you will have. If, deep down, you expect to flounder in failure, what can possibly motivate you toward success?

Optimistic perspectives work in similar fashion. If you expect personal growth from your participation in the economy, then your mind will create ideas that will bring about those opportunities.

Your urge to invest in yourself comes from a belief in a positive future – that you will reap the benefits of your effort whether with the purchase of an education, a company's stock, or a new computer for the office.

Let's say you give up hope of becoming a heart surgeon.

You come to this decision because you believe that you do not have the fine motor skills necessary to be successful in this profession, or that once you have mastered heart surgery, you figure no one will need your services. You decide not to make the effort to master heart surgery, and the community now has one less heart surgeon. Or, what if, on the island, you felt insufficient and lacked the self-confidence needed to manufacture shelters or believed that nobody would want your brand of shelters? Maybe you would have decided to look for nuts rather than invest time in the design and manufacture of shelters. Then the whole island community would lose the chance to have your type of shelter.

Each of these cases applies to the community as a whole. If large groups of people feel pessimistic about the outcome of their investments, the economic future will answer in kind, becoming what the community expects it to become.

Pessimism, like optimism, spreads through our interactions with others. When we slow down our self-investment, we slow down production, because there are less qualified people producing. When our investment and production activities decrease, we have fewer job opportunities. Fewer jobs leads to less income. Since production has slowed, we have less goods to consume, and consumption slows.

Today's modern economy is not the island. There are hundreds of thousands of businesses buying and selling from each other and paying for our services as we work. Investment and optimism drive the process forward as companies use the drives to advance, serve, and exchange to their advantage.

When pessimism and lack of investment send this process backwards, you must do two things if you are to engage and assert your skills. *First, maximize your chances of not being touched by these periods of pessimism by holding high, positive expectations no matter what the circumstances present.*

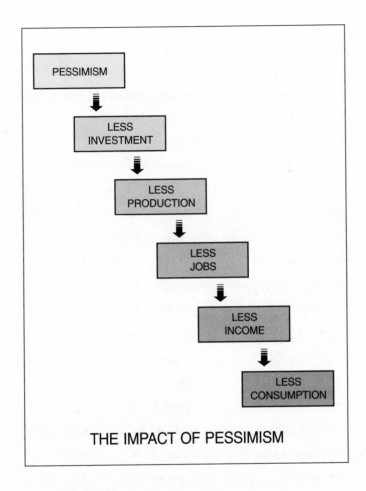

THE IMPACT OF PESSIMISM

Continue to be useful, productive, and of service to those you meet and in all situations in which you find yourself. *Second, always prepare for the future.*

Always invest in yourself. Be known as forward-looking and hopeful, a seeker of solutions. Others in depressed times will flock to you and respect you if you can remain confident and act on that faith.

Periods of stagnation have always occurred during the upward climb of the economy, and they will occur in the future. Nonetheless, all past depressions have been overcome. All have been met with stronger gains of economic success than in the past. This process is inevitable. After all, the striving for economic renewal and well-being is part of the human spirit.

How do you increase your personal productivity and economic well-being?

Remember:

❧ Investment is the time and effort taken with calculation to improve the future.

❧ At the heart of all your investments are your positive expectations.

❧ When it comes to investment, your use of time

becomes critical.

❦ Your effective investments in body and mind will distinguish you.

❦ Through education, you learn skills that provide you with abilities and usefulness that command a value in the eyes of others.

❦ Investing in yourself connects you with the community, and your investments help sustain the growth of the economy.

❦ If we expect personal growth and opportunity from our participation in the economy, then our minds will create ideas and actions that will bring about that personal growth and opportunity.

❦ Always invest in yourself. Be known as forward-looking and hopeful, a seeker of solutions.

## THE SPIRIT OF PERSONAL ECONOMICS CHECKLIST

✓ You have begun to invest in your body and your mind through exercise, healthy eating, a positive attitude, and education.

✓ You will continue to think positively about the future, even when others do not.

## WHAT'S NEXT?

In the next chapter, you will discover the benefits of selling your skills and personality. You will learn how selling can be the key to enjoying the Spirit of Personal Economics.

# 6

## SELL YOUR TALENTS
## IN THE MARKET
## OF OPPORTUNITY

A S YOU WORK TO ESTABLISH a lifestyle for yourself, you create your place in the economy.
Furthermore, when you release your creative energy
in your drives to advance, serve, and exchange, you
place yourself on the constructive side of human
relations. And when you combine this energy with
investments in the self and increase your usefulness

to others, you solidify your grasp of economic success.

## NOT THE
## TYPICAL SALES PITCH

We come now to selling. In the act of selling, you put the resources within you, the skills you have mastered, or the goods and services you possess to the test. In doing so, you will discover whether or not you have created value that rewards you and gives you a strong personal economy. To do this, simply place your skills, goods, and services before the community in the best possible light.

Selling comes naturally to us, not necessarily the type of selling that requires aggressive badgering, but the type where we sell our services and our ideas to the world and create value for others to enjoy.

Virtually everyone feels satisfaction from possessing a trait, quality, skill, or material good that others find useful. How you make what you have to offer attractive to others will determine how you pass the test of selling. So how do you accomplish all this?

## Acquire the Proper Perspective

Would it not serve you well if you could provide a good or service for which others would gladly exchange favors or money? Would it not increase your self-respect if you saw that others appreciated your talents and used them to increase their feelings of satisfaction? For most people, the answers to these questions would be yes. *For you to increase your economic well-being, you must feel that your life will improve (and it will) when you provide a quality good or service to others.*

## Offer a Quality Product or Service

In selling, the quality of the product or work effort that you offer is essential. If you offer a faulty product, no one will buy it.

## PUT YOUR
## BEST FOOT FORWARD

Your success in selling will depend on how you sell the product. To maintain momentum, you must put your best foot forward whenever you sell. You must:

❀ Abide by the heartfelt faith that you offer a unique product or service the world will want.

❀ Act on this faith whether you offer a product whose benefits must be continuously described to clients or whether you offer your time and efforts on a job.

❀ Cooperate and communicate with others honestly and intelligently.

Every time you interact with other people, you have a chance to sell your talents and personality. You want to make a successful impact at every opportunity. When you treat all people you meet with respect and interest, you improve your chances of passing the test of selling.

Determine the needs of others and serve them. The needs of people will always provide you with an abundance of economic opportunities.

## ACTIVITIES

➡ NOTICE HOW YOU INTERACT WITH PEOPLE AND HOW THEY INTERACT WITH YOU. ARE YOU ALWAYS POLITE? DO YOU SHOW AN INTEREST IN WHAT THEY SAY? DO YOU GET FRUSTRATED EASILY AND ACT RUDELY? ASK YOURSELF, "HOW CAN I IMPROVE THE WAY I SELL MY PERSONALITY AND SKILLS TO OTHERS?"

➡ FOR A DAY, PRETEND AS THOUGH YOUR LIFE WERE A TV PROGRAM IN WHICH CAMERAS FOLLOWED YOU AROUND ALL THE TIME. HOW WOULD YOU ACT IF MILLIONS OF PEOPLE WITNESSED EVERY MOMENT? HOW WOULD YOU TREAT PEOPLE KNOWING THAT WHAT YOU SAID AND HOW YOU SAID IT HAD ADDED WEIGHT AND VALUE? HOW WOULD YOU POSITIVELY IMPACT SOMEONE ELSE? RECORD HOW THE DAY WENT.

When you seek a job, describe a product with which you are entrusted, or talk to someone, you must maintain a positive attitude. Let your personality glow in the encounter. Let your investments in yourself pay off as you display your acquired expertise and go the extra mile in a spirit of determined usefulness. Repeat to yourself two fundamental questions: *"What do others want from me that may help their circumstances? And how can I provide answers that are useful to the situation at hand?"*

Do not confuse selling yourself with proving yourself. If you sell yourself successfully by deed, act, and productive result, you prove yourself automatically. Your usefulness is apparent. On the other hand, proving yourself may take the form of grandstanding, bragging, or "name dropping." Most people resent this behavior. Deep down, we feel an antipathy toward exaggeration. Why? The joy of working is serious business. The person who exhibits confidence, integrity, honesty, and who can "deliver the goods" will be successful in the eyes of others without having to draw on outside proof.

The American presidents, George Washington and Abraham Lincoln, were modest in disposition. Integrity shone in their deeds. For this reason, their countrymen admired them. Just think how many times you have heard someone cite integrity as high praise or lack of integrity as a fault. Integrity counts! If you put a positive, honest attitude in everything you do, the world will beat a path to your door. Salesmanship is an integral part of enjoying the Spirit of Personal Economics.

## SELLING CONNECTS US

So let's take another look at selling, particularly how it allows us to connect to our community. You will see that for you, for a company in which you work, or for the community in which you live, selling products and services is essential.

When people are willing to buy your community's output (the products your community creates and exports), it means that your community's work, business skills, and resources make the economy of your community competitive. For the community to continue being competitive, the community must have competitive business enterprises. And for businesses to be competitive, *you* must be competitive. This is why investment in the self is key to economic well-being. When you keep competitive in your ability to sell your knowledge, experience, skills, and products, you connect with your community and add value to it.

In selling, you join the age-old quest for economic prowess. It is key to the survival of a business enterprise just as it is the basis of your own well-being. All through this journey, discovering the Spirit philosophy, you have learned the importance of your decisions in making your economic destiny work for you.

In the end, the community will measure your personal economic success by your ability to sell yourself and add value to the community.

In order to capture a deeper sense of economic well-being through salesmanship, remember:

＊ In the act of selling, you put the resources that

are within you, the skills you have mastered, or the goods and services you possess to the test.

* To sell, acquire the proper perspective, offer a quality product or service, and put your best foot forward by cooperating and communicating honestly and intelligently.

* Abide by the heartfelt faith that you offer a unique product or service the world will want.

* The person who exhibits confidence, integrity, honesty, and who can "deliver the goods" will be successful in the eyes of others without having to draw on outside proof.

* If you put a positive, honest attitude in everything you do, the world will beat a path to your door.

* For the community to be competitive, the community must have competitive business enterprises. And for businesses to be competitive, *you* must be competitive.

❧ The community will measure your personal economic success by your ability to sell yourself.

## THE SPIRIT OF PERSONAL ECONOMICS CHECKLIST

✓ You've begun to see that by being yourself, acting honestly, and providing something that truly helps others, you can earn your keep and create value for your community.

# Epilogue

## THRIVING WITH THE SPIRIT OF PERSONAL ECONOMICS

YOUR CONFIDENCE IN THE OPPORTUNITIES that await you, your commitment to a constructive role in the community, and your desire to be of service to others will fill you with the Spirit of Personal Economics, the way of thinking that leads to a more satisfying economic well-being. In catching the Spirit, you've learned:

❧ How to delight in the material world.

❧ How the economy functions and why we have so many wonderful choices of products and services.

❧ How you connect to the community as producer and consumer.

❧ How goals are of vital importance.

❧ How a positive attitude empowers your efforts to gain economic well-being.

❧ How your drives to advance, serve, and exchange are deep impulses ready to help you.

❧ How to make a virtue of your work.

❧ How we rely on technology to improve our lives.

❧ How taking care of your own well-being can make a positive impact on solutions to world issues at the same time.

❧ How to invest in yourself.

❧ Ultimately, how selling your talents to the community earns your place in the market of opportunity.

Check out the diagram below to see a summary of your journey to catch the Spirit:

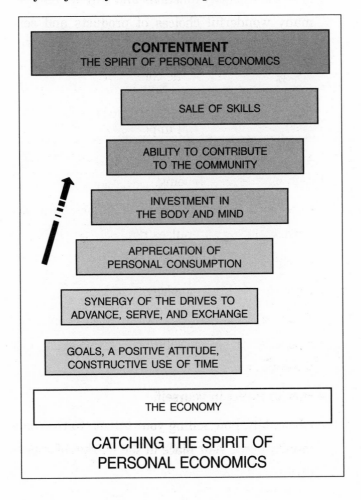

## THE TIME IS NOW!

*Never lose sight of the fact that you cannot watch this process from the sidelines.* You are one of the creators of talents and products to sell. You have the power to determine the quality of the goods and services that are produced. *Your ability to thrive will depend on your success in selling what you offer the world, either in skills, time on a job, or products.*

As investors, producers, marketers, and consumers, each of us determines a personal economic destiny. For our economic destiny to be successful, we must feel empowered to strive for that success.

You must have confidence in your journey. You must strive to go the extra mile at every step of the journey through life. Your confidence will feed your desire for self-improvement, inventiveness, entrepreneurship, competitiveness, and your rising standard of living. Your confidence will create your material world from dreams!

The time is now! Catch the Spirit of Personal Economics and proceed toward greater personal economic joy, purpose, and happiness!

# INDEX